Phoebe's Birthday

By Joanna Johnson
Illustrated by Eric Johnson

SLATE
FALLS
PRESS

Slate Falls Press, LLC
P.O. Box 7062
Loveland, CO 80537
www.slatefallspress.com

Library of Congress Cataloging-in-Publication Data Johnson, Joanna.
Phoebe's Birthday / by Joanna Johnson illustrations by Eric Johnson
ISBN 978-0-578-10560-4 ISBN 0578-10560-8
Library of Congress Control Number: 2012907988
Signature Book Printing, inc.
www.sbpbooks.com
Printed in the U.S.A.

for our grandparents

The summer that Phoebe turned six, she went to the seaside with her mother, father, grandma, grandpa, and baby brother. They stayed at their special vacation house, which was an old toy boat that had washed up on the beach.

Every morning after breakfast, Phoebe went out to the beach to play. She liked to gather shells and splash at the edge of the ocean. But she didn't know how to swim, and didn't like going out too far into the water.

Every afternoon, Phoebe's father tried to teach her how to swim. He held her up by her tummy while she practiced floating, but she always kept her one big toe on the bottom of the sea where she could feel the sand.

One morning, Phoebe's grandma took her for a special trip into town. As they walked up the path, she gave Phoebe a small red lollipop, and told her that it would take them just as long to walk to town as it would take Phoebe to eat her lollipop.

Grandma was right- just as Phoebe got to the stick of her lollipop, they arrived at the shop. This was a special shop, as it had a lot of fun things to look at.

When they got inside, Grandma explained that she would like to knit a dress for Phoebe's birthday, and asked Phoebe if she could decide what color she wanted the dress to be.

Phoebe knew right away that she wanted a pink dress. Pink was definitely her favorite color. The shopkeeper climbed up a tall ladder to get the pink yarn for Grandma.

Every afternoon, Phoebe practiced swimming with her father. But no matter how many times he asked her to, she was just too scared to float all by herself. Phoebe's friends came to visit, and they were very good at swimming. They liked to jump in the waves and even dive under the water. But not Phoebe.

The following afternoon, she decided to rest instead of practicing her swimming. She found her favorite quilt, which looked like rows and rows of colorful spools of thread, and snuggled up in the boat house. She drifted off to sleep for a little while...

...and dreamed she was swimming way out in the deep part of the ocean with the flying fish, splashing and dipping under the water without being afraid at all!

But when she woke up, she was just the same little mouse as before. That night, while they were working on a big puzzle, her mother reminded her that tomorrow was her sixth birthday.

The next afternoon, Phoebe decided to try swimming with her father again. He helped her to float, and asked her one more time to try to swim on her own. She floated, almost, then suddenly realized she had picked her toe up from the sand and she was really swimming all by herself! Her whole family cheered for her.

She swam all afternoon, and as the sun began to set, her mother wrapped her in a big towel and hugged her. Phoebe felt tired but proud. It was time to celebrate!

Phoebe's family sang "Happy Birthday" to her, and she ate a big piece of cake. And then she opened a box from her Grandma that had the beautiful pink knitted dress inside. She decided that she would always remember that very special day, and the summer they spent at the beach- the summer that she turned six.

the end

Phoebe's Sun Romper

Size Girl's size 1 [2, 3, 4] shown in size 4

Chest circumference 21" [21½", 22½", 23"]

Yarn Brown Sheep Cotton Fleece, 80% cotton, 20% wool; 215 yards per 100 gram skein.

MC Hawaiian Sky, 2 skeins; CC Celery Leaves, 1 skein

Needles US size 5 16" circular needles; US size 6 16" and 24" circular needles; US size 6 dpns

Notions 2 stitch markers, 3 stitch holders, 1 yard of 1/8 inch elastic cord

Gauge 20 sts over 4 inches in stockinette stitch on size US 6 needles

Pattern Notes This vintage-style sun romper is worked from the bottom up, and uses the same design element on the bodice as does the tunic. The legs are worked separately, then joined together and the garment is worked in the round. The contrast color ruching is worked in the round, then back and forth before casting off and working the i-cords straps for the neck. The only seam to finish is the grafting at the join where the legs meet. There is no casing for the elastic on the legs; it is woven through the ribbing at the lower part of the leg hem.

Leg:

Using size 6 16" needle and CC, CO 114 [120, 126, 132] sts. Being careful not to twist sts, join for working in the round and place marker. Knit 5 rounds.

Change to MC yarn and * k1, k2tog * repeat across round. 38 [40, 42, 44] sts dec. 76 [80, 84, 88] sts rem.

Switch to size 5 needles and work in k2, p2 ribbing for 4 rnds.

Place last 8 sts of round onto a stitch holder. Leaving a 16" tail for grafting later on, cut yarn. Place remaining stitches on a spare needle or waste yarn.

Repeat instructions for other leg, except do not cut the yarn.

Bodice:

Switch to US size 6 24" circular needle, and k 34 [36, 38, 40] sts, pm for new beginning of rnd, k 34 [36, 38, 40] sts, join second leg and knit around, joining to work in the round. 136 [144, 152, 160] sts.

Work st st in the round (knit every round) for 7 [7½, 8, 9] inches.

Work decrease round, switching to shorter needle if necessary.

Size 1 only: k2, then, *k2, k2tog* 16 times, then, k2. Repeat once more. 32 sts dec. 104 sts rem.

Size 2 only: * k2, k2tog * repeat from * to * across round. 36 sts dec. 108 sts rem.

Size 3 and [4] only: k2tog 1 [2] times * k2, k2tog * repeat from * to * 18 times, k2tog 1 [2] times, repeat once more 40 [44] sts dec. 112 [116] sts rem.

Continue knitting as instructed for all sizes:

Purl 1 rnd. Work st st in the round (knit every round) for 2, [2½, 2¾, 3] inches.

Leaving MC yarn attached, switch to CC yarn and k 1 rnd, p 1 rnd two times. Leaving a 12" tail for weaving in, cut CC yarn.

Switch to MC yarn and k 1 rnd.

Increase round: kfb every stitch across rnd. 208 [216, 224, 232] sts. Knit 5 rnds.

Decrease round: k2tog across rnd. 104 [108, 112, 116] sts rem.

13(14,15,16)"

21(21.5, 22,23)"

27(29,30,32)"

Leaving a 12" tail for weaving in, cut MC yarn and switch to CC yarn. Knit 1 rnd.

Create buttonholes:

First round: p 62 [65, 68, 70] sts, BO 3, p 26 [26, 26, 28], BO 3, p 10 [11, 12 ,12].

Next round: k 62 [65, 68, 70] sts, CO 3, k 26 [26, 26, 28], CO 3, k 10 [11, 12 ,12].

Bind off for back: P 42 [44, 46, 48] sts, BO 62 [64, 66, 68] sts pw. Remove marker. BO 10 sts pw, placing final st from right hand needle onto left hand needle. 32 [34, 36, 38] sts rem.

Leaving a 12" tail for weaving in, cut CC yarn. Begin working back and forth. Turn work so wrong side is facing, switch to MC yarn, and p 1 row.

Increase row (RS): kfb every stitch across rnd. 64 [68, 72, 76] sts. Work 5 rows in st st, beginning and ending with a purl row.

Decrease row (RS): k2tog across rnd. 32 [34, 36, 38] sts rem.

Leaving a 12" tail for weaving in, cut MC yarn and switch to CC yarn. Turn work so right side is facing and knit 4 rows.

Knit 4, place on holder, BO across row to last 4 sts.

Straps: Switch to dpns and work an i-cord strap on the last 4 stitches for 16 [18, 20, 22] inches. Repeat for other side using 4 sts from holder.

Finishing Graft stitches from one holder to the next at the top of the leg ribbing. Weave in all ends. Block. Cross straps in back, thread through buttonholes, and tie in a bow.

Gather Leg: On the inside of the romper, thread elastic cord through the leg ribbing every two stitches, using the knit stitches as a threading guide. Tie off elastic where it seems appropriate, with a circumference of about 10-12" per leg. This will allow for the simple adjusting of the leg when the garment is fitted.

Phoebe's Sun Tunic

Size Girl's size 2 [4, 6, 8, 10, 12] shown in size 6

Chest circumference 22½" [23", 24", 25½", 27", 29"]

Yarn Brown Sheep Cotton Fleece, 80% cotton, 20% wool; 215 yards per 100 gram skein.

MC Majestic Orchid, 2 [2, 2, 2, 3, 3] skeins

CC Prosperous Plum, 1 skein

Needles US size 6 24" circular needles; US size 6 dpns; sizes 2-6 also require US size 6 16" circular needles

Notions 4 stitch markers

1 stitch holder

Gauge 20 sts over 4 inches in stockinette stitch on size US 6 needles

Pattern Notes This sweet summer top is a seamless knit worked from the hemline up. The contrast color ruching on the bodice is worked in the round, then back and forth, before casting off at the neckline and working i-cord neck straps. The straps slip through buttonholes, which are located on the back of the tunic, and easily tied into a pretty bow, which also allows for a custom-fit width throughout the bodice.

Using CC, CO 140 [148, 156, 168, 180, 192] sts.

Being careful not to twist sts, place marker and join for working in the round.

Work 6 rows in garter st (k 1 rnd, p 1 rnd.)

Switch to MC yarn, and work in st st (knit every rnd) for 2 [2, 3, 3, 4, 4] inches.

Place markers for decreases as follows: k2, pm, k 66 [70, 74, 80, 86, 92], pm, k4, pm, k 66 [70, 74, 80, 86, 92], pm, k2.

Decrease row: k2, sl m, ssk, k to 2 sts before next marker, k2tog, sl m, k4, sl m, ssk, k to 2 sts before next marker, k2tog, sl m, k2. 4 sts dec. 136 [144, 152, 164, 176, 188] sts rem.

Knit 7 rnds.

Work decrease rnd every 8th rnd 6 [7, 8, 9, 10, 11] times more, switching to short needles as necessary. 112 [116, 120, 128, 136, 144] sts rem.

Knit 1 rnd, leaving beginning of round marker in place, and removing markers for side decreases.

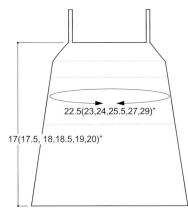

22.5(23,24,25.5,27,29)"

17(17.5, 18,18.5,19,20)"

Leaving MC yarn attached, switch to CC yarn and k 1 rnd, p 1 rnd twice.

Leaving a 12" tail for weaving in, cut CC yarn. Switch to MC yarn and k 1 rnd.

Increase round: kfb every stitch across rnd. 124 [132, 240, 256, 272, 288] sts. Knit 5 rnds.

Decrease round: k2tog across rnd. 112 [116, 120, 128, 136, 144] sts rem.

Leaving a 12" tail for weaving in, cut MC yarn and switch to CC yarn. Knit 1 rnd.

Create buttonholes:

First round: P 68 [70, 72, 78, 82, 88] sts, BO 3, p 26 [28, 30, 30, 34, 34], BO 3, p 12 [12, 12, 14, 14, 16].

Next round: K 68 [70, 72, 78, 82, 88] sts, CO 3, k 26 [28, 30, 30, 34, 34], CO 3, k 12 [12, 12, 14, 14, 16].

Bind off for back: P 46 [48, 50, 53, 57, 60] sts, BO 66 [68, 70, 75, 79, 84] sts pw. Remove marker. BO 10 [10, 10, 11, 11, 12] sts pw, placing final st from right hand needle onto left hand needle. 36 [38, 40, 42, 46, 48] sts rem.

Leaving a 12" tail for weaving in, cut CC yarn.

Switch to MC yarn, turn work so wrong side is facing, and p 1 row.

Begin working back and forth.

Increase row (RS): kfb every stitch across rnd. 72 [76, 80, 84, 92, 96] sts.

Work 5 rows in st st, beginning and ending with a purl row.

Decrease row (RS): k2tog across rnd. 36 [38, 40, 42, 46, 48] sts rem.

Leaving a 12" tail for weaving in, cut MC yarn, switch to CC yarn, turn work so right side is facing, and knit 4 rows.

Knit 4, place on holder, BO across row to last 4 sts.

Straps: Switch to dpns and work an i-cord strap on the last 4 stitches for 18 [18, 20, 20, 22, 22] inches. Repeat for other side using 4 sts from holder.

Finishing Weave in all ends. Block. Cross straps in back, thread through buttonholes, and tie in a bow.

Phoebe's Party Dress

Size Girl's size 2 (4, 6, 8, 10, 12)

Chest Circumference 22½" [24", 26", 27½", 29", 30½"]

Yarn Brown Sheep Cotton Fleece, 80% cotton, 20% wool; 215 yards per 100 gram skein. Shown in size 4 (Provincial Rose) and size 10 (Sunflower Gold.)

4 [4, 5, 6, 7, 8] skeins.

Needles US size 6 24" circular needles; sizes 2 and 4 also require US size 6 16" circular needle

Notions Stitch marker, waste yarn, spare circular needle for joining yoke, optional:1 yard of 1/8 inch elastic.

Gauge 20 sts over 4 inches in stockinette stitch on size US 6 needles

Pattern Notes This sweet and simple dress is a seamless project worked from the hem up. The scallop lace hem is knit, then the stockinette stitch skirt. All sizes use a multiple of four stitches in the skirt section, so feel free to knit the skirt in a different stitch, such as double seed, cat's eye, or mini cable. After dividing for the front and back, a bit of short row shaping is worked at the neckline. (The pattern uses the simplest form of short row shaping, which does not employ the wrap and turn method, since the shaping is neatly covered by the lace yoke at the neck.) The dress waits patiently on scrap yarn while you cast on and knit the lace yoke, and then you attach the yoke to the dress by sliding the dress into the center of the yoke and knitting them together at the neckline. This dress was designed to be a summer garment, but would be just lovely knit in wool for a winter jumper, too.

Using longer circular needle, cast on 252 [270, 288, 306, 324, 342] sts. Being careful not to twist sts, place marker and join for working in the round.

Knit one round. Purl one round. Knit one round.

Begin working the six-row scallop lace pattern as follows:

Rnd 1: * k1, yo, k2, ssk, k2tog, k2, yo * repeat from * across rnd.

Rnd 2: Knit

Rnd 3: * yo, k2, ssk, k2tog, k2, yo, k1 * repeat from * across rnd.

Rnd 4: Knit

Rnd 5: Purl

Rnd 6: Knit

Work the six-row lace pattern a total of 3 [4, 5, 5, 6, 7] times.

Then, work rnds 1-3 of pattern once.

Decrease rnd: * k1, k2tog* repeat from * across rnd. 84 [90, 96, 102, 108, 114] sts dec. 168 [180, 192, 204, 216, 228] sts rem.

Purl 1 rnd.

Begin working in st st (knit every row) and work straight without shaping for 8 [9½, 11, 13, 15, 17] inches, (measuring from the purl round.)

Decrease rnd: * k1, k2tog * repeat from * to * across rnd, switching to shorter needles as necessary. 56 [60, 64, 68, 72, 76] sts dec. 112 [120, 128, 136, 144, 152] sts rem.

Purl one round.

Bodice: Work straight without shaping in st st for 3¾ [4½, 5¼, 6, 6½, 7] inches.

Divide for Front and Back:

Back: BO 3 sts, knit 53 [57, 61, 65, 69, 73] sts.

Leaving other half of bodice stitches live on the needle, you will now be working back and forth in rows. Turn work and BO 3 sts, purl across row to BO sts from previous row. 50 [54, 58, 62, 66, 70] sts rem.

BO 2 sts, k across row to BO sts. 48 [52, 56, 60, 64, 68] sts rem.

BO 2 sts, p across row to BO sts. 46 [50, 54, 58, 62, 66] sts rem.

BO 2 sts, k across row to BO sts. 44 [48, 52, 56, 60, 64] sts rem.

BO 2 sts, p across row to BO sts. 42 [46, 50, 54, 58, 62] sts rem.

K1, ssk, k to last 3 sts, k2tog, k1. 40 [44, 48, 52, 56, 60] sts rem.

Work without shaping in st st for 10 rows.

Short row neck shaping:

P8, turn, sl 1, k7.

P6, turn, sl 1, k5.

P4, turn, sl 1, k3.

P across row.

K8, turn, sl 1, p7.

K6, turn, sl 1, p5.

K4, turn, sl 1, p3.

Knit one row.

Purl one row.

40 [44, 48, 52, 56, 60] sts rem.

Place sts on scrap yarn. Cut yarn.

Front: Repeat as for back.

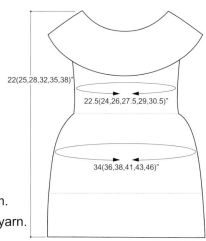

22(25,28,32,35,38)"

22.5(24,26,27.5,29,30.5)"

34(36,38,41,43,46)"

Yoke: Using longer circular needle, CO 171 [180, 189, 207, 216, 225] sts.

Knit one round. Purl one round. Knit one round.

Resume working in the scallop lace pattern, working the six-row repeat a total of 3 [3, 3, 4, 4, 4] times.

Then, work rounds 1-3 of the pattern once more.

Decrease rnd: * k1, k2tog * repeat from * to * across rnd, switching to shorter needle as necessary. 57 [60, 63, 69, 72, 75] sts dec. 114 [120, 126, 138, 144, 150] sts rem.

Join yoke to dress.

Slip yoke over top of dress, being sure that the wrong side of the yoke is placed upon the right side of the dress bodice.

Working on the lace yoke, knit 17 [16, 15, 17, 16, 15] sts. This is the arm opening. Then, knitting one stitch from the yoke together with one stitch from the front bodice, k2tog 40 [44, 48, 52, 56, 60] times. Working again on the lace yoke only, knit 17 [16, 15, 17, 16, 15] stitches. Then knitting one stitch from the yoke together with one stitch from the back bodice stitches, k2tog 40 [44, 48, 52, 56, 60] times. BO all sts knitwise.

Finishing Weave in ends. Block. Optional: work a single crochet edge around the armhole openings. Optional: Thread elastic along the underside of the dress neckline, just inside the neck edge, gather to fit, secure.

Phoebe's Headwrap

Size Girl's size 2 [4, 6, 8, 10, 12] Head circumference 15" [16", 17", 17½", 18½", 19"]

Yarn Brown Sheep Cotton Fleece, 80% cotton, 20% wool, 215 yards per 100 gram skein.

Shown in size 4: MC Hawaiian Sky, 35 yards; CC Celery Leaves, 15 yards.

Shown in size 8: MC Majestic Orchid, 35 yards; CC Prosperous Plum 15 yards.

Needles For sizes 2 and 4, US size 5 9" circular needles; for sizes 6-12, US size 5 16" circular needles

Notions 1 stitch marker

Gauge 19 sts over 4 inches in stockinette stitch on size US 5 needles

Pattern Notes This feminine headwrap can be worn as either a headband, as pictured on the younger model, or as a flapper-style wrap, as seen on the older model. It is a quick accessory, worked in the round, and embellished with a fun flower in a contrasting color.

Headwrap Using MC, CO 76 [80, 84, 88, 92, 96] sts. Being careful not to twist stitches, place marker and join for working in the round.

K 1 rnd, P 1 rnd. Repeat once more.

K 13 [14, 15, 16, 17, 18] rnds.

P 1 rnd, K 1 rnd. Repeat once more. BO all sts pw.

Flower Using CC, CO 128 sts.

Working back and forth, knit 1 row, purl 1 row, knit 1 row.

Switch to MC, and k2tog across row. 64 sts rem.

Purl 1 row. K2tog across row. 32 sts rem.

Purl 1 row. K2tog across row. 16 sts rem.

Purl 1 row. K2tog across row. 8 sts rem.

Knit 1 row. K2tog across row. 4 sts rem.

K2tog twice. 2 sts rem. K2tog. Tie off last stitch.

Finishing Curl flower into a spiral and stitch the flower onto the headwrap as shown, gathering it a bit as you stitch the flower on. Weave in ends. Block.

abbreviations

beg	beginning	pfb	purl in front & back of stitch
BO	bind off	pw	purlwise
CC	contrast color	rem	remain
CO	cast on	rnd	round
dec	decrease(d)	rs	right side
dpn	double-pointed needle	sl	slip
k2tog	knit two together	sl m	slip marker
k	knit	ssk	slip, slip, knit
kfb	knit in front & back of stitch	st	stitch
MC	main color	sts	stitches
p	purl	st st	stockinette stitch
patt	pattern	ws	wrong side
pm	place marker	yo	yarn over

Phoebe's Spool Quilt

I designed this quilt based on a traditional quilt block, adding gray strips between rows to create the look of a shelf stacked with brightly colored spools. All of the fabric prints are a part of Amy Butler's Soul Blossoms line, and the solids are from her line of coordinating solid fabrics. This versatile design is a great way to showcase your favorite fabric prints.

Block Size 10"

Finished Quilt Size 55" X 59"

Seam Allowance 1/4"

Note

There are 20 spool blocks in the quilt, requiring a total of 20 6 ½ x 6 ½ spool centers. I cut 2 spool centers from each of the following 10 fabrics:

Peacock Feathers in Blush
Disco Flower in Chocolate
Dancing Paisley in Lemon
Delhi Blooms in Grass
Twilight Peony in Amaranth
Peacock Feathers in Bright Pear
Temple Tulips in Azure
Delhi Blooms in Lime
Disco Flower in Tangerine
Temple Tulips in Cinnamon

You can easily cut six center spool squares from a fat quarter of fabric.

	YARDAGE	FABRIC	CUT
Spool Center	*See note	Soul Blossoms prints	20- 6 ½" X 6 ½"
Spool Caps	1	Solid Copper	40- 10 ½" X 2 ½"
Spool Background	1 ¼	Solid Ivory	40- 6 ½" X 2 ½"
			80- 2 ½" X 2 ½"
Shelf Strips	1 ¾	Solid Slate	6- 1 ½" X 42"
			2- 1 ½" X 58"
Border	1 ¾	Peacock Feathers in Sea Glass	4- 7" X 60"
Binding	1	Delhi Blooms in Rose	
Back	3 ½	Twilight Peony in Azure	

ASSEMBLY

1. Sew one spool background rectangle to each side of the spool center. Press seams toward the center.

2. Sew one spool background square to each end of the spool cap at a 45 degree angle and trim corners as shown. Press seams toward spool cap.

3. Sew one end cap to the top and bottom of each spool as shown, being sure to line up the spool end cap with the center square. Press seams toward spool cap.

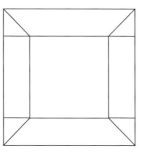

4. Make five rows of spools, having four spools in each row.

5. Join the 5 rows of spools, placing a 42" shelf strip between each row as shown in the diagram to the right. Sew a 42" shelf strip to the top of the first row and to the bottom of the last row. Sew the 58" shelf strips to the sides as shown.

6. Sew a border piece to each side of the quilt, trim. Sew final border pieces to top and bottom of the quilt as shown.

7. Quilt and bind using your preferred method. (I chose to hand quilt my quilt. For the binding, I used 2 ¾" strips of fabric folded in half.)

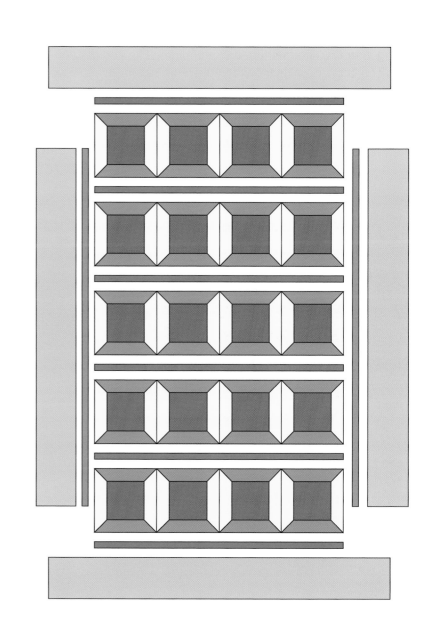

40

For a nicely textured vintage look to your quilt, machine wash and dry your fabrics before cutting. Use a cotton batting, quilt using your favorite method, and machine wash and dry your finished quilt to create a subtle puckered effect.

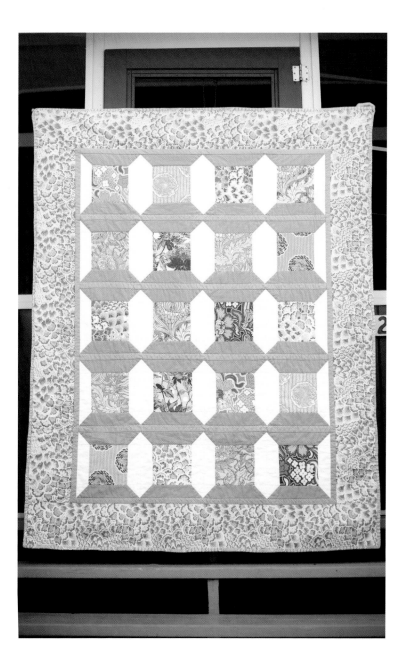

Phoebe Mermouse

We dreamed up the idea for a sewn mermouse doll in the early planning stages of this book. Amy Butler's bright fabrics are a perfect match for this fun softie. Created from only five pattern pieces, she is simple enough for a young sewist to stitch with just a little help from an grown-up. The finishing touches- buttons, shells, ribbons... are the most fun of all. I used a child's shell bracelet for her necklace. Have fun being creative with the details!

Finished size: 18" tall

Cutting Instructions

Trace pattern pieces onto paper and cut them out neatly.

Cut the ear, arm, and head/torso pieces from the ivory fabric, transfer markings for placement of ears and arms. Transfer the markings for the eyes, nose, and belly button onto the front head/torso piece.

Cut the halter top.

For the tail piece, fold the fabric with wrong sides together before pinning on the pattern piece, and cut through both layers of fabric.

Cut 2 ears out of quilt batting.

Use a 1/4" seam allowance throughout as you begin sewing your project.

Materials List

Amy Butler Ivory fabric, fat quarter (for the head/torso, ears, arms)

Amy Butler Peacock Feathers in Seaglass, 9" X 22" fabric piece (for the tail)

Amy Butler Temple Tulips in Cinnamon, 5" X 8" fabric piece (for the halter top)

DMC Embroidery Floss in # 603 (pink) and # 938 (brown)

2 brown buttons, 5/8" (for the eyes)

1 pink heart button (for the nose)

1 pink felt button (for the belly button)

1 pink rose button, 1 1/2" (for the hair accessory)

2 squares of quilt batting, about 3" X 3" each (for the ears)

Toy stuffing of your choosing

2 yards of 1/8" satin ribbon in teal

1. With wrong sides together, sew head/torso to tail at the waistline. Press seam toward tail. Make 2, one for the front and one for the back.

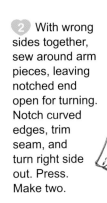

2. With wrong sides together, sew around arm pieces, leaving notched end open for turning. Notch curved edges, trim seam, and turn right side out. Press. Make two.

3. Lay two ear pieces wrong sides together. Place one batting ear on top, sew around ear, leaving open on short straight end for turning. Notch curved edges, trim seam, and turn right side out. Press. Make two.

4. Using pink embroidery thread, work blanket stitch around edge of each ear.

5. Stitch eyes, nose, and belly button to front of doll with coordinating embroidery thread, using marking guides from the pattern piece. Embroider eyelashes.

6. Stuff arms. Using notches for placement, baste arms to right side of the front of the doll, crossing arms across tummy, as shown.

7. Using markings for placement, baste ears to right side of the front of the doll, as shown.

8. With right sides together, stitch the front of the doll to the back of the doll, keeping ears and arms folded inside, and leaving doll open between markings on the tail for turning. Notch curved edges, clip corners, trim seams. Turn doll right side out, press.

9. Stitch the tail through both layers along the curve as marked.

10. Stuff doll through opening. Close opening with a ladder stitch, or stitch of your choice.

11. Narrow hem all four sides of the halter top. Attach a 12" piece of ribbon to each corner as shown.

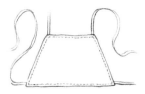

12. Help Phoebe Mermouse tie on her shirt, stitch or safety pin the flower button and ribbon near her ear, and put on her necklace. Now it's time to play!

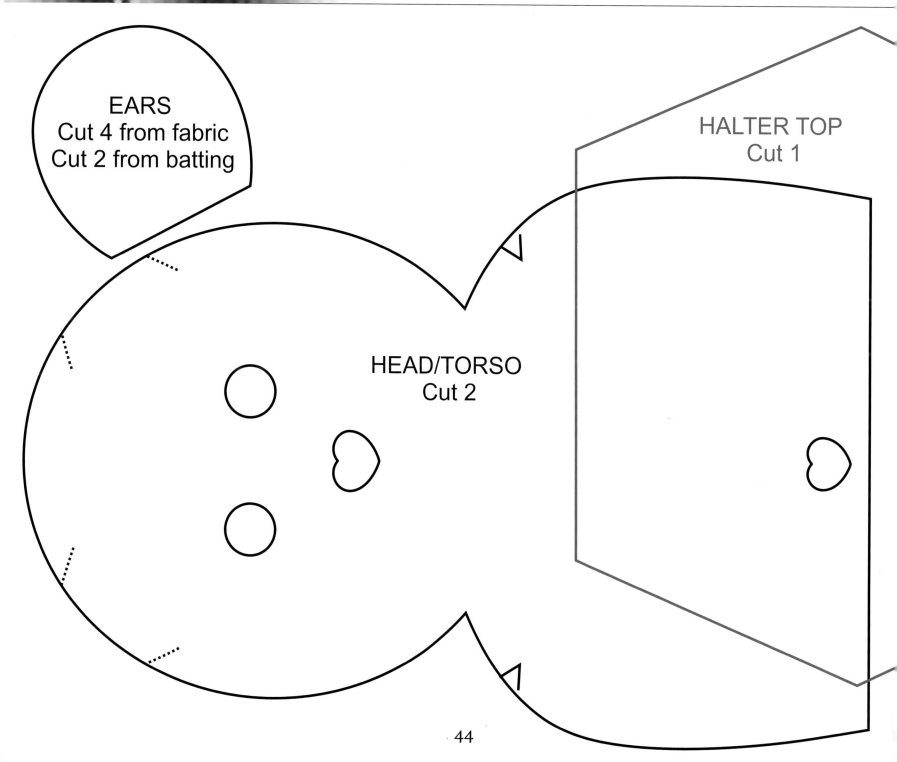

EARS
Cut 4 from fabric
Cut 2 from batting

HALTER TOP
Cut 1

HEAD/TORSO
Cut 2

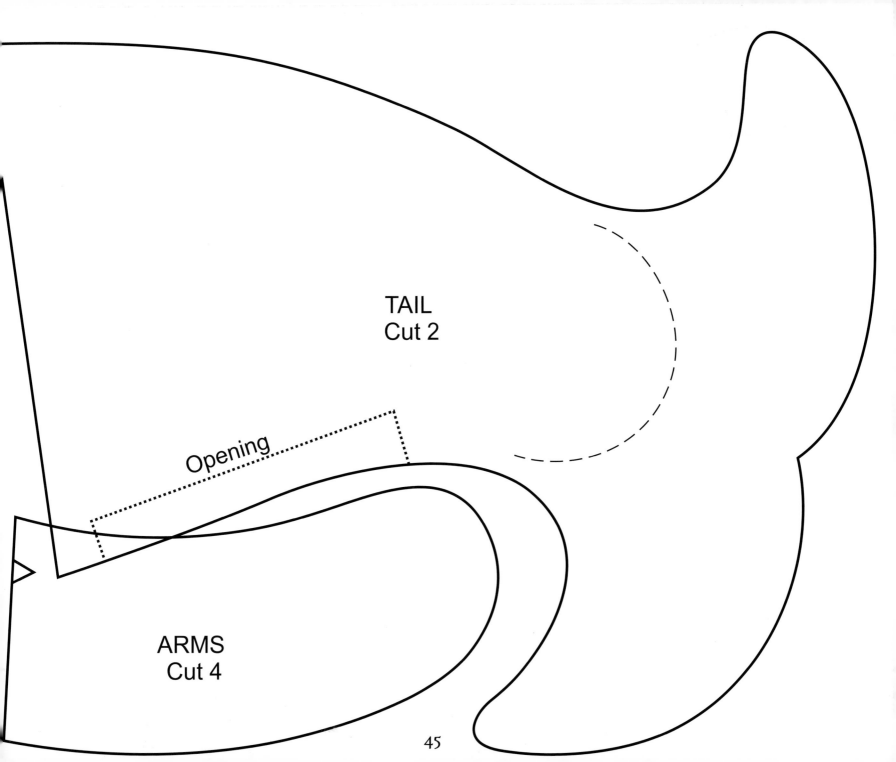

TAIL
Cut 2

Opening

ARMS
Cut 4

45

Eric, 1976

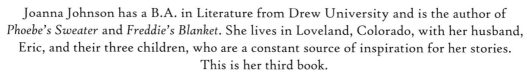

Joanna Johnson has a B.A. in Literature from Drew University and is the author of *Phoebe's Sweater* and *Freddie's Blanket*. She lives in Loveland, Colorado, with her husband, Eric, and their three children, who are a constant source of inspiration for her stories. This is her third book.

Eric Johnson has been working in commercial design for two decades as a signwriter, muralist, and graphic designer. He has enjoyed returning to his childhood love of drawing by setting pencil to paper to illustrate this book. He lives with his wife, Joanna, and their three children in Loveland, Colorado. This is his third book.

Joanna, 1978

Yarn
Brown Sheep Co, Inc.
100662 CR 16
Mitchell, NE 69357
phone 800.826.9136
brownsheep.com

Fabric
Amy Butler Design
122 S. Prospect St.
Granville, OH 43023
phone 740.587.2841
amybutlerdesign.com

Deepest thanks to: Our family, friends, and readers, for their encouragement and love. Peggy Jo Wells and the wonderful staff at Brown Sheep Company, for offering yarn support and for their kindness. Amy Butler, for offering fabric support and for her enthusiasm for this project. Christa Tippmann, for another amazing series of photographs. Hadley Austin, for being a wonderful and patient tech editor. Megan Helzer, our copyeditor and sample knitter, for her watchful eye. Karen DeGeal, our sewing pattern editor, for her helpful ideas. Yvonne and Gordy, for allowing us to photograph the knits at their lovely beach. Fancy Tiger Crafts in Denver, for inspiring our story's yarn and fabric store, and for hosting the photo shoot at their pop up shop at the Makerie in Boulder. Our models: Chloe Tippmann, Laurel Johnson, Piper Holt, Shiloh Bruce, and Sydney Tippmann, for being so sweet and fun. Out test knitters: Christa Tippmann, for her friendship; Erin McLaughlin, for her thoughtfulness; Evangeline Snyder, for her passion; Joyce Bensen, for everything (thanks, Mom!); Karen DeGeal, for her wisdom; Krista Elston, for her kindness; Megan Helzer, for her care; Molly Henthorne, for joining in the fun; and Pam Miller, for her smile. Our sewing pattern testers: Karen DeGeal, for her expertise, and Amelia Chapman, for staying up late. We are thankful for our three children who enrich our lives so very much, and to God for leading, inspiring, and loving us.